Meat Recipe Bo

A Cookbook to Show How to Make High Protein Meaty Dishes

BY: Ivy Hope

IVY HOPE
COOKBOOK

Copyright/License Page

Table of Contents

Introduction.. 7

Fish.. 9

    Bass Bake 10

    Fish Biryani 12

    Bacon-wrapped Hake Parcels.................................... 15

    Baked Trout with Rice Stuffing 17

    Salmon Macaroni-and-Cheese Pie 20

    Coriander Swordfish Steaks 22

    Scandinavian-style Fish Pie 24

Beef... 26

    Cheese-filled Beef Patties 27

    Beef Pie 29

    "Spaghetti" and Meatballs...................................... 32

    Roast Beef in Vodka 35

    Beef Curry 38

    Oxtail Stew... 41

Beef Stew in Black Beer with Mustard Herb Dumplings 44

Pork 47

Sage Infused Pork Chops 48

Quick Pork Pie 50

Gammon Roast with Cranberry Glaze 52

Pea and Ham Soup 54

Pork Burger Patties 56

Belly of Pork with Beer and Onions 58

Red Onion and Chorizo Sausage Tart 60

Ham Quiche 62

Bacon and Onion Flan 64

Sausage Casserole 66

Lamb 69

Durban Lamb Curry 70

Tomato Bredie 73

Lamb Hotpot with Cheese Scone Topping 76

Rack of Lamb 79

Lamb Koftas 81

Minted Roast Leg of Lamb with Mustard Seeds..84

Lamb Shanks in White Wine 86

Simple Lamb Casserole...88

Leg of Lamb with Haricot Beans 90

Lamb and Aubergine Lasagne..93

Chicken 96

Tandoori Chicken..97

Cape Malay Chicken Curry...99

Chicken with Peas and Bacon 102

Chicken Korma 104

Beer and Chicken Pies...107

Parsley and Parmesan Crumbed Chicken..110

Sweat and Sour Chicken with Stick Rice..112

Bonus Recipes...114

Duck with Orange Marmalade Glaze...115

Ostrich Pie..117

Cassoulet 120

Conclusion 123

About the Author 124

Author's Afterthoughts 125

Introduction

This book has been written to provide just over forty recipes and an essential entry into cooking meat dishes. You might be a beginner wanting to learn how to prepare and cook meat, but the recipes also provide more advanced techniques as well.

If you are a beginner, you will need to realize that the basic oven, stovetop, pots, and pans are necessary before continuing. Alternatively, you will need to become a bit creative to finish each recipe successfully.

The book is formatted in a no-nonsense way so that each recipe is easily followed. The book is divided to separate the types of meat being used, and then has a bonus chapter to finish things off. There are also images to help visualize the way the dish should look once the meal is on the table.

Fish

Bass Bake

Serving Size: 4

Cooking Time: 30 Minutes

Ingredients:

- 1 Lb fresh bass, in 4 equal portions
- salt and pepper to taste
- ½ Cup butter, melted
- ½ Cup white wine
- ½ oz peppercorns
- 2 Cups heavy whipping cream
- 4 Tbsp Dijon mustard

Instructions:

1. Clean, skin and debone the bass. Place the portion of fish in a baking pan and season with salt and pepper.

2. Add the melted butter and half the wine.

3. Cover with tin foil and bake at 356°F until cooked through, about 15 to 20 minutes.

4. Place peppercorns, the rest of the wine, the heavy whipping cream and Dijon mustard into a saucepan. Then, cook over medium heat, stirring, until the sauce has thickened.

5. Spoon sauce over the bass and serve.

Fish Biryani

Serving Size: 4-6

Cooking Time: 1 Hour 20 Minutes

Ingredients:

- ¼ Cup oil
- 2 large onions
- 4 cardamom pods; 4 whole cloves; 2 pieces cinnamon bark
- 1 tsp fresh ginger; 4 cloves garlic
- 1 tsp each fennel seeds, ground coriander and ground cumin
- 2 tsp biryani masala
- 8 baby potatoes
- 2 Lb fresh hake, cubed
- salt and pepper
- 2 Cups basmati rice
- 1 can (15 oz) brown lentils
- handful parsley, chopped
- grated zest on 1 lemon

Instructions:

1. Heat the oil in a pot, slice in the onions and fry them until they are soft.

2. Chop the ginger and crush the garlic. Add in the cardamom, cloves, cinnamon bark, ginger and garlic and then fry them up for a couple of minutes.

3. Add the fennel, cumin, coriander, masala and a splash of water and mix to form a paste.

4. Peel and cut baby potatoes into ½ inch thick disks, then add and fry until coated in spice.

5. Next, cover the pot with the lid and simmer until potatoes begin to soften.

6. Season fish with salt and pepper and add to pot. Steam for 10 to 15 minutes until fish is firm and opaque. Set aside.

7. Place rice in a pot with 3 cups of water. Add salt and boil until it's tender. Then drain the rice through a colander.

8. Drain and rinse the lentils, then stir them into the rice.

9. Layer rice and fish mixture in a pot.

10. Add ¼ cup water and cover with the pot lid. Simmer it for 30 minutes.

11. Top the biryani with parsley and lemon zest.

Bacon-wrapped Hake Parcels

Serving Size: 4

Cooking Time: 30 Minutes

Ingredients:

- 4 (5 oz) hake portions
- salt and pepper
- ½ packet (16 to 24 oz) ends & pieces bacon
- 1 box small tomato's
- 1 packet (6 oz) baby spinach
- 2 cloves garlic, chopped
- olive oil

Instructions:

1. Season hake, lay two rashers bacon on a chopping board and top with a hake portion. Fold bacon over fish.

2. Place same side down in an ovenproof dish. Repeat with the remaining bacon and fish.

3. Place cherry tomatoes around fish.

4. Bake at 464ºF for 15 minutes, until bacon is crisp and hake is cooked through.

5. Sauté spinach and garlic in a glug of oil and season.

6. Serve fish parcels and veg with rice.

Baked Trout with Rice Stuffing

Serving Size: 4

Cooking Time: 1 Hour 10 Minutes

Ingredients:

- 4 trout
- 1 Tbsp lemon juice, salt and pepper to taste
- rub inside the trout with lemon juice and salt and pepper
- For the stuffing:
- 1 onion, finely chopped
- 1 clove garlic, crushed
- 2 oz butter
- 1 Tbsp vegetable oil
- ½ Cup rice; ½ cup boiling water
- 1 Tbsp almonds; 1 Tbsp sultanas
- To bake:
- butter; lemon juice; salt and pepper
- ½ Cup white wine

Instructions:

1. First, sauté the onion and the garlic in the butter and oil. When golden brown, add the rice and cook until shiny and golden, taking care not to burn the rice. Then, season with salt and pepper. Add a half cup of boiling water. Cover and cook gently until the water is absorbed and the rice is almost cooked through.

2. Chop the almonds and toss lightly in butter with the sultanas. Stir the sultanas and the nuts into the rice stuffing.

3. Lay the trout in a well buttered baking dish, score sides, and rub well with butter, lemon juice and salt and pepper. Then, pour a little white wine into the dish.

4. Cover with tin foil and bake at 320°F for 20 minutes.

5. Lastly, remove the foil and bake for a further 5 minutes.

Salmon Macaroni-and-Cheese Pie

Serving Size: 6-8

Cooking Time: 55 Minutes

Ingredients:

- 4 eggs
- 2 cans macaroni-and-cheese sauce
- 1 can salmon chunks
- 1 ½ Cups bread crumbs, no crust
- 1 Cup grated mature cheddar cheese
- ¼ tsp salt

Instructions:

1. First, beat the eggs in a bowl. Stir in the macaroni-and-cheese sauce, salmon chunks, soft bread crumbs, grated cheese and salt.

2. Then, pour the mixture into a greased baking dish.

3. Do not cover and bake for 40 to 45 minutes at 356ºF till set.

Coriander Swordfish Steaks

Serving Size: 4

Cooking Time: 32 Minutes

Ingredients:

- ½ Cup butter
- 2 Tbsp fresh coriander, chopped
- 1 Tbsp parmesan, grated
- 4 swordfish steaks
- 1 Tbsp olive oil
- 4 zucchini (courgettes), cut into long slices
- 1 red pepper, gartered

Instructions:

1. Preheat barbecue to high. Cream the butter until soft. Then, add the coriander and parmesan. Mix to combine, press into a butter pot and set aside.

2. Lightly oil barbecue grill bars, brush fish steaks with oil, place on grill bars and cook 34 minutes each side according to thickness.

3. Brush vegetable with oil and place on grill, cook for 3 to 4 minutes until golden.

4. Serve vegetable and swordfish topped with a dollop of coriander butter.

Scandinavian-style Fish Pie

Serving Size: 4

Cooking Time: 40 Minutes

Ingredients:

- 1 onion, chopped
- 2 cloves garlic, minced
- 2 Tbsp butter
- 2 Tbsp flour
- 2 Cups milk, warmed
- 1 ¾ Lb cubed fish
- 1 Cup frozen pea
- zest of 1 lemon
- 1 Tbsp dill, chopped
- 3 potatoes

Instructions:

1. First, fry onion and garlic in butter until soft. Sprinkle over flour and fry for another 2 minutes.

2. Stir in milk. Add cubed fish and cook until firm.

3. Add frozen peas and lemon zest. Sprinkle over dill.

4. Spoon into an ovenproof dish.

5. Grate potatoes and squeeze excess fluid from potato. Season and sprinkle over pie.

6. Brush with melted butter and bake at 356°F for about 10 to 20 minutes, until potato is crisp and pie is heated through.

Beef

Cheese-filled Beef Patties

Serving Size: 4 large patties

Cooking Time: 45 Minutes

Ingredients:

- 1 ⅓ Lb lean minced beef
- 1 Tbsp barbecue sauce
- 2 Tbsp tomato sauce
- 1 small onion, finely chopped
- ¼ Cup mature cheddar, grated
- 4 ½ oz crushed pineapple, drained

Instructions:

1. Preheat barbecue to a medium heat or make braai to medium heat. In a large bowl, place beef, barbecue sauce, tomato sauce and onion, and mix to combine. Shape beef mixture into 8 patties, flattening slightly with the palm of your hand.

2. Top 4 patties with cheese and pineapple, then cover with remaining patties, carefully moulding edges of patties together to form 4 large patties.

3. Cook patties on lightly oiled barbecue for 10 minutes each side.

Beef Pie

Serving Size: 4-6

Cooking Time: 1 Hour 20 minutes

Ingredients:

- ⅓ Cup oil
- 2 celery stalks, chopped
- 3 carrots, chopped
- 2 Cups small onions
- 3 cloves garlic, finely chopped
- 4 ½ Lb beef cubes, dusted with ¼ cup flour
- 1 Cup beer
- 1 ½ Cups beef stock
- ½ Lb sliced button mushrooms
- 1 Tbsp tomato puree

Instructions:

1. Heat oil in large deep pot. Add celery, onions and garlic and soften gently.

2. Dust beef cubes with flour, turn up heat and add to pot.

3. Brown only a few cubes at a time to avoid the pot losing heat and the meat stewing before it is browned. Put aside browned cubes.

4. Once all cubes are browned, put all cubes back in pot.

5. Add the beer and stock. Then, cover the pot and turn the heat down to allow the meat to simmer gently for an hour, adding extra stock if the mixture starts to dry out.

6. Add mushrooms, tomato puree, ground cloves, salt and pepper and simmer for 20 minutes.

7. Thicken the gravy if necessary, with butter and flour.

8. Next, place mixture in a pie dish and cover with the rolled-out pastry, trimming and crimping edges neatly.

9. Brush with egg and bake at 356°F until golden brown for about 15 to 20 minutes.

"Spaghetti" and Meatballs

Serving Size: 4

Cooking Time: 55 Minutes

Ingredients:

- 1 Lb beef mince
- 1 onion, chopped
- 3 Tbsp breadcrumbs
- 1 egg, whisked
- 1 Tbsp Dijon mustard
- 2 Tbsp fresh basil, nicely chopped or 2 tsp dried mixed herbs
- salt and pepper
- 3 Tbsp butter
- 2 cloves garlic, chopped
- 2 tsp lemon juice
- 1 can tomato puree
- ½ Cup water or stock
- 1 Tbsp sugar
- 2 Lb large baby marrows, sliced into strips

Instructions:

1. Combine mince, onion, breadcrumbs, egg, mustard and herbs. Season well.

2. Shape into 12 to 14 golf-ball-sized meatballs and chill for 20 minutes.

3. Place meatballs, butter, garlic and lemon juice in a deep microwave-safe dish and microwave on high for 3 minutes.

4. Add tomato puree, water and sugar, and microwave for another 3 to 4 minutes, stirring at one-minute intervals. Season and set aside.

5. Place baby marrow strips in a large bowl with ¼ cup water and cover with clingfilm.

6. Microwave on high for 1 to 2 minutes. Drain and rinse.

7. Serve "spaghetti" with meatballs and sauce, and garnish with basil leaves.

(You can swap marrow strips for regular spaghetti)

Roast Beef in Vodka

Serving Size: 6-8

Cooking Time: 2 Hours 15 Minutes

Ingredients:

- 4 ½ Lb sirloin or beef roast
- 1 Tbsp coarse salt
- 2 Tbsp ground peppercorns
- 3 Tbsp parsley
- 3 Tbsp thyme
- 3 cloves garlic, crushed
- 2 Cups vodka spirit
- ¼ Cup olive oil
- 2 Tbsp vegetable oil
- 4 Tbsp unsalted butter

Instructions:

1. Rub the seasoning into the roast. Place in a zipper plastic bag, and add the parsley, 2 tablespoons of thyme, the garlic, the vodka spirit and olive oil. Refrigerate for 3 days to marinate. Let it stand for 2 hours after taking it out the refrigerator before cooking.

2. Heat the oven to 356°F. Remove from the bag, reserving the marinade.

3. Add the vegetable oil and sear the meat on all sides in a hot skillet, 4 to 6 minutes. Transfer the meat to a baking pan.

4. Insert a cooking thermometer into the roast, and roast in the oven for about 1 ½ hours, until the thermometer registers 131°F for medium-rare.

5. Transfer the meat to a chopping board and let it rest, for at least 20 minutes, reserving the cooking juices.

6. Just before serving, pour the cooking juices and marinade into a saucepan and heat gently. Mix in butter and season with salt, pepper and remaining thyme. Strain the sauce and discard the herbs.

Beef Curry

Serving Size: 4

Cooking Time: 1 Hour 25 Minutes

Ingredients:

- 1 tsp coriander powder
- 1 tsp cumin powder
- 1 Lb cubed beef
- 4 Tbsp vegetable oil
- 1 onion, peeled and chopped
- 1 tsp garlic, crushed
- 1 tsp ginger, crushed
- 1 tsp chilli powder
- 1 tsp sugar
- 2 tomatoes, chopped
- 1 Cup water
- 1 tsp salt

Instructions:

1. Mix the coriander and the cumin powders with the beef cubes and leave to stand.

2. Pour oil into a pan, turn to a medium heat and fry the onion until golden brown.

3. Add the garlic, the ginger and the chilli powder and stir fry for a few minutes, certainly taking care that the mixture does not burn.

4. Add the sugar and the beef and cook until it is nicely browned but do not allow to burn.

5. Add the tomatoes and water and stir until all the ingredients blend together.

6. Simmer for about 45 minutes with the lid on, adding a little water if necessary.

7. Add the salt and cook for a further 15 minutes.

8. Serve with freshly boiled rice and accompaniments such as tomato and onion sambal, bananas in milk or yoghurt and chutney.

Oxtail Stew

Serving Size: 4

Cooking Time: 2 Hours 35 Minutes

Ingredients:

- 2 Tbsp olive oil
- salt and pepper
- 3 Lb oxtail
- 2 onions, chopped
- 4 cloves garlic, sliced
- 5 sprigs rosemary; 5 sprigs thyme
- 2 bay leaves
- 1 Cup red wine
- 2 tsp Worcester sauce
- 1 can chopped and peeled tomatoes
- 1 tsp ground cloves
- 6 cups beef stock
- 2 punnets baby carrots
- 1 punnet fine green beans
- 1 punnet button mushrooms

Instructions:

1. First, heat oil in a heavy bottomed pot until smoking hot.

2. Season meat well and brown all over. Set aside.

3. Sauté onions for 5 minutes or until softened. Add garlic and herbs and cook for another minute.

4. Deglaze pan with wine and cook for a minute.

5. Return meat to pot. Add Worcester sauce, tomatoes and cloves.

6. Pour in stock, cover and simmer for 2 hours or until meat is tender.

7. Add carrots, green beans and mushrooms and simmer for 10 to 15 minutes or until cooked through.

8. Serve with mashed potatoes.

Beef Stew in Black Beer with Mustard Herb Dumplings

Serving Size: 6-8

Cooking Time: 3 Hours 15 Minutes

Ingredients:

- 2 ¼ Lb stewing beef, cubed
- 2 Tbsp flour; 3 Tbsp oil
- 3 onions, peeled and sliced
- 4 carrots
- 2 celery sticks, sliced
- 1 Tbsp fresh thyme, copped; 2 Tbsp fresh parsley, chopped
- 2 Cups beef stock
- 2 Cups black beer
- 1 Tbsp sugar
- 1 Tbsp Worcestershire sauce
- 1 bay leaf; 1 tsp salt
- 3 ½ oz self-raising flour
- 1 ¾ oz fresh bread-crumbs
- 1 ¾ oz shredded lard
- 2 tsp mustard seeds (optional)
- 2 Tbsp chopped mixed herbs

Instructions:

1. Coat the meat with flour. Brown the beef.

2. Add the onions and fry until soft. Slice the carrots and then add celery, herbs, and stock with beer. Allow to boil, while stirring it continuously.

3. Add the sugar, Worcester sauce and the bay leaf. Cover the pan cook the beef on low heat until tender for about 2 hours, and then season with salt.

4. Mix together the flour, breadcrumbs, lard, mustard seeds and herbs to make dumplings. Add about ⅓ cup water and mix till it becomes a dough-like mixture. Make into eight balls.

5. Add to the beef, cover and cook for 15 to 20 minutes until the dumplings are fluffy and risen.

6. Tip: do not lift the lid until 15 minutes has passed and be careful not to cook on too high a heat and check regularly as this dish catches quite easily.

Pork

Sage Infused Pork Chops

Serving Size: 4

Cooking Time: 25 Minutes

Ingredients:

- 4 pork chops
- olive oil
- a few sage leaves
- salt and pepper
- 4 rosemary sprigs

Instructions:

1. First, rub the pork chops with a little olive oil and season.

2. Place one or two sage leaves on each chop and place in a hot pan, leaf side down for 4 minutes, then turn and cook until golden.

3. The sage imparts a fantastic flavour to the meat.

4. Fatty rind of the chops can be removed and salted and baked in the oven until crisp.

5. Serve dressed with rosemary sprigs

6. Enjoy with mash and a green salad.

Quick Pork Pie

Serving Size: 4

Cooking Time: 50 Minutes

Ingredients:

- 2 Tbsp oil
- 1 large onion, finely chopped
- 3 cloves garlic, finely chopped
- 1 Lb cubed pork
- flour for coating pork cubes
- 1 Tbsp fresh sage leaves, chopped
- 3 ½ Tbsp dry sherry
- 2 tsp Dijon mustard
- ½ Lb button mushrooms, finely sliced
- 2 Cups good vegetable stock
- 1 roll readymade puff pastry

Instructions:

1. First, heat oil in a pan. Then, add onion and garlic. Fry until soft.

2. Coat the pork cubes in the flour, add to the pan and fry until golden brown.

3. Add sage, sherry, 1 cup of vegetable stock, mustard and mushrooms and cook gently for 15 to 20 minutes.

4. Next, If the mixture is too dry, add a little vegetable stock to create a moist consistency.

5. Place the mixture into a 7-inch pie dish and cover with the rolled-out sheet of pastry. Trim off any excess and crimp edges of pastry.

6. Brush with egg and bake at 356ºF for 15 to 20 minutes or golden brown.

Gammon Roast with Cranberry Glaze

Serving Size: 6-8

Cooking Time: 5-6 Hours

Ingredients:

- 3 Lb gammon roast
- ½ Gallon apple juice
- ½ Gallon cranberry juice
- 1 tsp Italian herbs
- 2 Tbsp cranberry jelly or jam
- 1 clove garlic, finely chopped

Instructions:

1. First, place the gammon in a large pot and boil gently in the fruit juices and dried herbs for around 4 to 5 hours.

2. Remove from the liquid and carefully remove the skin, leaving as thick a layer of fat at possible.

3. Next, in a small saucepan, place the honey and cranberry jelly or jam, and heat until the ingredients blend together to form a syrupy liquid that can be painted on with a brush.

4. Add finely chopped garlic and glaze the gammon with the mixture.

5. Place in a moderate oven until nice and golden, around an hour, basting as necessary.

6. Enjoy as a Sunday roast with roast vegetables.

7. Tip: The next day use the bones and any leftover meat as a base to make a delicious pea and ham soup.

Pea and Ham Soup

Serving Size: 4

Cooking Time: 2 Hours 15 Minutes

Ingredients:

- 8 Cups chicken stock
- leftover meat and bone from a pork roast
- 1 cup split-peas
- ½ cup of lentils
- 1 Lb frozen peas
- salt and pepper to taste
- ½ Cup cream

Instructions:

1. First, in a large pot, bring the chicken stock to the boil.

2. Add any leftover meat and bone from a pork roast and simmer for half an hour.

3. Add a cup of split peas and a half cup of lentils.

4. Simmer for another 30 to 45 minutes, stirring regularly.

5. Next, add the frozen peas and continue to simmer for 30 minutes.

6. Remove the bone and blitz contents of pot with a hand held blender until smooth.

7. Taste and adjust seasoning. Add ½ Cup cream and allow to stand for 5 minutes off the heat.

Pork Burger Patties

Serving Size: 4

Cooking Time: 35 Minutes

Ingredients:

- 1 Lb coarsely minced pork
- 1 cup breadcrumbs
- 1 tomato, grated
- 1 onion, grated
- 1 tsp salt
- 1 pinch mixed herbs
- 1 pinch sage
- freshly ground black pepper
- 1 egg
- oil for frying

Instructions:

1. In a bowl, combine all the ingredients firstly and mix well. If you find the mixture too wet add more breadcrumbs.

2. Heat oil in a non-stick pan. Form the burger patties and fry gently until just cooked through and golden, about 3 minutes on each side.

3. Serve on a crispy bun with tomato, lettuce and onion rings.

4. Enjoy with a dollop of Dijon mustard or your favourite sauce.

Belly of Pork with Beer and Onions

Serving Size: 6-8

Cooking Time: 2 Hour 45 Minutes

Ingredients:

- Cake flour
- salt and freshly ground black pepper
- 4 ½ Lb belly of pork, rolled and secured with string
- oil for frying
- 1 ¼ Cups beer
- 12 small (picking) onions, skinned and parboiled
- ½ Lb baby carrots, cleaned
- 3 stalks celery, chopped
- ¼ Lb bacon, diced

Instructions:

1. Salt and pepper the cake flour.

2. Coat the pork in flour and then brown it in a heated pan or pot. Pour off the fat. Heat the beer and sugar together in a pan.

3. Pour 2 Tbsp of the mixture over the pork, coat the pork evenly.

4. Place the pot lid and reduce to a simmer.

5. Simmer for 2 to 2 ½ hours or until the meat is tender.

6. Pour a little of the beer mixture over the meat when necessary and turn the meat regularly.

7. Add parboiled onions to the meat with the carrots, celery and bacon and let them cook with the pork for about an hour.

8. Remove the string and carve.

Red Onion and Chorizo Sausage Tart

Serving Size: 4

Cooking Time: 40 Minutes

Ingredients:

- 1 red onion, finely chopped
- 1 tsp brown sugar
- 1 roll readymade puff pastry
- 1 chorizo sausage
- 1 egg, beaten
- salt and pepper

Instructions:

1. In a small pot fry onion and sugar gently with a little olive oil until soft and just starting to caramelise.

2. Second, unroll the puff pastry sheet and place onto a baking sheet. Make an incision with a knife all around the pastry rectangle, about ½ inch in from the edges, but do not actually cut all the way through. (Alternatively, form them into smaller pies in a cake dish).

3. Spread the onion mixture onto the pastry, taking care to keep it inside the lines.

4. Slice the sausage thinly and arrange on top of the onion mixture.

5. Lastly, crush the edges of the pastry with the egg and bake at 356°F until golden brown, approximately 15 to 20 minutes.

(The filling is very versatile, and you can add anything else you choose, such as olives or peppers)

Ham Quiche

Serving Size: 16 slices

Cooking Time: 1 Hour 10 Minutes

Ingredients:

- Readymade shortcrust pastry to line two 9-inch pie dishes
- 3 Cups chopped ham or any smoked meat or sausage of your choice
- ¼ Cup breadcrumbs
- 14 oz cheese of your choice or even a mixture
- 1 small onion, finely chopped
- 8 eggs
- 2 Cups whipping cream
- 1 ½ tsp salt
- ½ tsp sugar
- pinch cayenne pepper

Instructions:

1. Line pie dishes with pastry.

2. Mix ham, breadcrumbs, cheese and onion together. Spread evenly into the pie dishes.

3. Beat the eggs slightly. Then, add the remaining ingredients and beat again. Pour into the dishes.

4. Bake for 15 minutes at 428°F.

5. Reduce temperature to 356°F and bake a further 30 minutes or until mixture is set.

6. Let stand for 15 minutes before serving.

Bacon and Onion Flan

Serving Size: 6

Cooking Time: 1 Hour

Ingredients:

Pastry:

- 9 oz onions chopped
- 9 oz flour
- 3 ½ oz butter or margarine
- 1 pinch salt
- 3 ½ oz water

Bechamel sauce:

- ¼ Cup butter
- 2 oz flour
- 2 Cups milk
- 2 egg yolks
- 1 pinch salt, pepper and nutmeg
- 3 ½ oz lean smoked bacon, cut into strips

Instructions:

1. Prepare shortcrust pastry with flour, butter, salt and water, making sure not to overwork it.

2. Fry chopped onions in the butter or oil until lightly browned. Set aside.

3. Make a bechamel sauce: melt the butter, add the flour (do not brown) and then the milk (mixing well to prevent lumps forming), season and allow to cook.

4. Remove from the heat and add the egg yolks. Add the onions and adjust the seasoning.

5. Fry bacon strip gently until translucent.

6. Line the flan tin or pastry dish with the shortcrust pastry and fill to half the depth of the dish with the onion mixture. Arrange the bacon strips on top.

7. Bake at 410°F for 20 to 25 minutes.

8. Sprinkle on the nutmeg and serve very hot.

Sausage Casserole

Serving Size: 4

Cooking Time: 50 Minutes

Ingredients:

- 1 Tbsp oil
- 1 onion, peeled and sliced
- 2 cloves garlic, crushed
- 2 Tbsp chopped fresh sage
- 1 Lb pork sausages
- 1 yellow and 1 green pepper, seeded and sliced
- 1 can whole peeled tomatoes
- 1 Tbsp tomato puree
- 1 Tbsp cider
- 2 Tbsp cornflour
- 4 ½ oz mushrooms, sliced
- salt and pepper

Instructions:

1. First, heat the oil in a large casserole dish. Add onions and garlic and cook gently until tender. Remove from the pan and set aside.

2. Second, add the sausage to the pan and cook until evenly golden brown all over, about 10 minutes.

3. Remove the sausages from the pan. Then, add the peppers, cook for about 3 minutes. Return the sausages and onion to the pan.

4. Next, stir in the tomatoes with their juice, tomato puree and cider.

5. Then, cover and bake at 374°F for 30 minutes.

6. Mix the cornflour with a little water to make a paste and stir into the casserole together with the mushrooms, sage and seasoning about 10 minutes before the end of the cooking time.

Lamb

Durban Lamb Curry

Serving Size: 4-6

Cooking Time: 1 Hour 50 Minutes

Ingredients:

- 6 cloves garlic, finely grated
- 4 onions, sliced
- 3 chillies, halved
- 2 tsp each ground coriander and turmeric
- 1 ½ inch knob ginger, finely grated
- 2 Tbsp canola oil
- 3 bay leaves
- 3 sticks cinnamon
- 3 salad tomatoes, grated
- 1-3 tsp chilli powder
- generous pinch salt
- handful fresh coriander
- 10 fresh or dried curry leaves
- 1 ¾ Lb baby potatoes, halved
- 2 cups vegetable stock
- 1 ⅓ Lb stewing lamb or goulash
- 2 Tbsp hot curry powder
- 1 large packet tomato paste

Instructions:

1. First, heat oil in your pot and sauté onion for 5 to 8 minutes approximately or until soft and golden. Add ginger, garlic and chillies. Then, fry for a further 2 minutes.

2. Second, season meat and add to pot and brown all over. Add bay leaves, curry leaves and spices and fry until fragrant. Then, stir to coat meat with spices.

3. Next, stir in tomato paste, potatoes, salad tomatoes and stock. Adjust seasoning, then simmer on a low-medium heat for about 60 to 75 minutes approximately or until meat is soft (take care not to over stir, rather swirl pot occasionally).

4. Once meat is tender, stir in coriander. Lastly, serve curry with rice.

Tomato Bredie

Serving Size: 4-6

Cooking Time: 2 Hours 15 Minutes

Ingredients:

- 3 Tbsp olive oil
- salt and pepper
- 2 ¼ Lb lamb stewing meat (like knuckles)
- a little cornflour, for dusting
- 3 onions, chopped
- 4 cloves garlic, chopped
- 1 Tbsp smoked paprika (optional)
- ½ Tbsp ground coriander
- ½ tsp ground cloves
- 1 tsp chili flakes (optional)
- ½ cup red wine
- 2 cans chopped and peeled tomatoes
- 1 can tomato puree
- 1 Tbsp brown sugar
- 2 tsp soy sauce
- 1 Lb baby potatoes, halved
- ½ Cup beef stock

Instructions:

1. Heat oil in a heavy bottomed pot. Season meat and lightly dust with cornflour. Then, brown meat all over, remove and set aside.

2. Reduce heat and sauté onion for 5 minutes. Add garlic and sauté for a minute. Add spices and chilli flakes (optional) and cook for a minute until fragrant, adding a splash of oil if needed.

3. Return meat to pot and add wine to deglaze. Add tomato puree, chopped tomatoes, sugar and soy sauce.

4. Simmer for 1 hour, keeping pot half-covered.

5. Add potatoes and stock and cook for 30 to 40 minutes or until reduced.

6. Garnish with basil and vine tomatoes and serve with rice on the side.

Lamb Hotpot with Cheese Scone Topping

Serving Size: 4

Cooking Time: 2 Hours 15 Minutes

Ingredients:

- 3 Tbsp oil
- 3 Lb lamb, cubed
- 5 Tbsp seasoned flour
- zest and juice of 1 orange
- 2 ½ Cups red wine
- 1 Tbsp fresh rosemary
- salt and freshly ground black pepper
- Topping:
- ¼ Cup butter, diced
- 10 oz self-rising flour
- 3 ½ oz mature cheddar cheese, coarsely grated
- 2 Tbsp mixed fresh herbs, chopped
- 4 spring onions, finely chopped
- salt and freshly ground black pepper
- 2 Tbsp plain yoghurt
- 5 Tbsp water

Instructions:

1. Toss the lamb cubes in seasoned flour, shaking off any excess.

2. Heat the oil and fry the cubes in batches until the meat is browned. Return all the meat to your pan along with the orange zest and juice, red wine, rosemary and seasoning and cook for a minute.

3. Place all the meat in a pie dish, cover with tin foil and cook in the oven for 1 hour 30 minutes at 356°F.

4. Make the topping by rubbing the butter and flour together until mixture resembles breadcrumbs, then stir in the cheese, herbs, onions and seasoning.

5. Mix the yoghurt with the water and gradually add to the flour mixture to make a soft, pliable dough. Knead lightly on a floured surface. Next, roll out the dough until large enough to fit the top of the dish.

6. Take off tin foil, cut dough into either wedges or rounds and arrange on top of the meat.

7. Bake for a further 15 to 20minutes at 392°F.

Rack of Lamb

Serving Size: 2-4

Cooking Time: 2 Hours 40 Minutes

Ingredients:

- 2 racks lamb, trimmed
- 2 cloves garlic
- 4 Tbsp Dijon mustard
- 2 Tbsp soy sauce
- 1 tsp each of dried marjoram, rosemary and thyme
- ½ tsp ground ginger
- 2 Tbsp olive oil
- salt and pepper

Instructions:

1. First, place all ingredients except the lamb into a blender and pulse to form a thick paste.

2. Coat the racks with the paste and place on a baking rack to marinade for 2 hours at room temperature.

3. Roast racks in a pre-heated oven at 356°F for 30 minutes.

4. Serve with herbed mashed potatoes or roast vegetables.

Lamb Koftas

Serving Size: 12-14 koftas

Cooking Time: 2 Hours 35 Minutes

Ingredients:

- 1 Lb lamb
- 1 onion, quartered
- 4 fresh parsley sprigs
- 4 fresh coriander sprigs
- 2 fresh mint sprigs
- ½ tsp ground cumin
- ½ tsp mixed spice
- 1 tsp paprika
- salt and freshly ground pepper
- Mint Dressing:
- 2 Tbsp finely chopped fresh mint
- 6 Tbsp natural yoghurt

Instructions:

1. Roughly chop the lamb, place in a food processor and process until smooth. Transfer to a plate.

2. Add the onion, parsley, coriander and mint to the processor and process until finely chopped.

3. Add the lamb together with the spices and seasoning and process again until very smooth. Transfer to a bowl and chill for about 1 hour.

4. For the mint dressing, mix the ingredients together and chill.

5. Next, mould the meat into small sausage shapes and skewer with wooden or metal kebab sticks.

6. Preheat the grill and cook the koftas for 5 to 6 minutes, turning once.

7. Serve immediately on savoury rice with mint dressing in a bowl. Fresh crusty bread makes a good accompaniment.

8. Tip: soak wooden kebab sticks in water before baking.

Minted Roast Leg of Lamb with Mustard Seeds

Serving Size: 4-6

Cooking Time: 4-5 hours

Ingredients:

- 2 ¾ Lb leg of lamb
- 5 cloves garlic, sliced
- ½ Cup chicken stock
- ⅓ Cup fresh chopped mint
- 3 Tbsp white wine vinegar
- 2 Tbsp mustard seeds
- 3 Tbsp olive oil
- 3 Tbsp lemon juice

Instructions:

1. Preheat the oven to 338°F.

2. Second, place the leg of lamb in a roasting dish.

3. With a sharp knife make incisions in the leg approximately 2cm apart and insert a slice of garlic in each slit.

4. Pour the stock over the lamb.

5. Mix together the mint, vinegar, mustard seeds, olive oil and lemon juice and rub mixture over the lamb.

6. Roast very slowly for 4 to 5 hours.

Lamb Shanks in White Wine

Serving Size: 4

Cooking Time: 2 Hours 30 Minutes

Ingredients:

- 2 Tbsp olive oil
- 4 lamb shanks
- 1 small onion, chopped
- 5 cloves garlic, sliced
- 2 tsp fresh rosemary, chopped and 2 sprigs for garnish
- salt and pepper to taste
- 1 Cup dry white wine

Instructions:

1. Braise the lamb shanks and set aside.

2. Reduce the heat and then add the garlic and onion, cook gently until translucent.

3. Return the shanks to the pan and add the fresh rosemary, salt and pepper.

4. Pour in the wine, then bring to a simmer. Cover with tightly fitting lid and simmer for 2 hours or until tender.

5. During cooking turn the shanks once or twice.

6. Serve garnished with the sprigs of rosemary.

Simple Lamb Casserole

Serving Size: 4

Cooking Time: 2 Hours 30 Minutes

Ingredients:

- 2 ¼ Lb lamb pieces, preferably neck, cut into small pieces
- 1 Lb carrots, sliced
- 2 onions, sliced
- 1 tsp mixed dried herb
- salt and pepper
- 1 Cup beer

Instructions:

1. Arrange pieces of meat, the carrots and onions in layers in a casserole dish.

2. Sprinkle on the herb and season with salt and pepper.

3. Add the beer and cook for 2 hours at 356°F.

4. Serve with baked potatoes in their jackets.

Leg of Lamb with Haricot Beans

Serving Size: 4-6

Cooking Time: 2 Hours 25 Minutes

Ingredients:

- 6 Lb leg of lamb
- 4 cloves garlic
- olive oil
- salt and pepper
- fresh or dried rosemary leaves
- 1 bay leaf
- 1 Lb dried haricot (small white beans), soaked in cold water
- 2 Tbsp butter
- ⅔ Cup lamb stock
- 2 Tbsp red wine
- watercress

Instructions:

1. Insert slivers of garlic into slits in the leg.

2. Rub down the lamb with olive oil. Then, season with salt and pepper. Sprinkle with rosemary.

3. Next, set the lamb on a rack in a shallow roasting tin, place in the oven and roast for approximately 2 hours at 356°F.

4. Rinse the beans and place in a saucepan with a generous covering of water. Then, add the remaining garlic and the bay leaf and bring to the boil.

5. Reduce heat and simmer for 45 minutes until tender.

6. Next, transfer the roast to a board and allow to stand, loosely covered, for 10 to 15 minutes.

7. Then, skim off the fat from the cooking juices, then add the wine and stock to the roasting tin. Boil over the medium heat, stir and scrape the base of the tin, until slightly reduced. Strain into a gravy boat.

8. Drain the beans, discard the bay leaf, then toss the beans with butter until it melts, and season to taste with the salt and pepper.

9. Lastly, garnish the lamb with the watercress and serve with the beans and sauce.

Lamb and Aubergine Lasagne

Serving Size: 4-6

Cooking Time: 3 Hours 45 Minutes

Ingredients:

For the meat sauce:

- ¼ Cup olive oil
- 2 ¼ Lb lamb brisket
- 1 large onion, finely diced
- ½ Cup chopped celery
- ½ Cup finely chopped carrot
- 2 tsp each dried oregano and basil
- 1 tsp dried rosemary
- 2 cloves garlic, crushed
- 2 cans peeled chopped tomatoes
- 1 small can tomato puree
- 2 bay leaves
- 3 Cups vegetable stock
- 1 Cup parmesan cheese
- salt and pepper
- 2-3 large aubergines, thinly sliced and salted
- 3 Cups fine breadcrumbs
- oil for frying
- 1 Lb feta cheese
- dried lasagne sheets
- 1 ¾ Cups bechamel sauce

Instructions:

1. First, prepare the meat sauce. In a large pan, heat the oil. Then, add the meat and braise until brown. Add a little stock and allow to simmer very slowly for around 2 hours. The meat should fall apart very easily.

2. Second, using your hands strip the meat from the bones and remove most of the fat and discard.

3. In a separate pot, in a little oil, cook onion, celery, carrots and herbs until soft then add the reserved meat.

4. Add the garlic, chopped tomato, tomato puree and bay leaves to the mix and a little of the stock. Then, cook for a few minutes approximately before adding the balance of the stock. Allow to simmer and reduce down to a runny but not too wet consistency.

5. Add the parmesan and set aside off the heat. Taste and adjust seasoning if necessary.

6. Pat the aubergine slices dry and dredge in the flour. Then, dip in the beaten eggs and in the crumbs. In a frying pan, heat the oil and pan-fry the aubergine slices. Drain on kitchen paper.

7. To assemble the lasagne, start by placing a layer of the meat sauce in the bottom of a lasagne dish. Crumble some of the feta over the meat then arrange a layer of aubergines on top followed by lasagne sheets and then bechamel sauce.

8. Repeat the process finishing off with bechamel sauce and cheese.

9. Bake at 356°F for 45 minutes until golden brown on top.

10. Tip: Use beef mince instead of lamb, to reduce time.

Chicken

Tandoori Chicken

Serving Size: 3-6

Cooking Time: 1 Hour

Ingredients:

- ½ Cup Greek style plain yoghurt
- 1 ½ tsp garam masala
- 2 cloves garlic, crushed
- 2 Tbsp lemon juice
- 2 Tbsp tandoori masala
- 2 Tbsp fresh coriander leaves, finely chopped
- 6 chicken thigh fillets, excess fat removed

Instructions:

1. First, combine the yoghurt, crushed garlic, tandoori masala, lemon juice, garam masala and coriander in a bowl and mix well.

2. Second, add the chicken, coat well, cover and refrigerate for at least 1 hour, or overnight if time permits.

3. Next, preheat a barbecue or char grill plate and lightly brush with oil. Then, cook the chicken, in batches if necessary, for 10 to 15 minutes on medium heat, turning the chicken once and basting with the remaining marinade, until golden and cooked through.

4. Serve on a bed of frilly lettuce with basmati rice and condiments of choice.

Cape Malay Chicken Curry

Serving Size: 4-6

Cooking Time: 1 Hour 35 Minutes

Ingredients:

- 2 Tbsp canola oil
- 2 onions, finely chopped
- salt and milled pepper
- 6 chicken drumsticks
- 4 chicken thighs
- 4 cloves garlic, finely grated
- 1 inch knob ginger, finely grated
- 1 ½ inch knob fresh turmeric, grated or ½ Tbsp ground turmeric
- 5 tsp each mild curry powder and garam masala
- 1 Tbsp each ground cumin and ground coriander
- sprig curry leaves
- 1 packet tomato paste
- 2 salad tomatoes, grated
- 1 can chopped tomatoes
- 6 medium potatoes, peeled and quartered
- 1 Cup chicken stock
- 1 can full cream coconut milk
- a few threads saffron (optional)
- 1 packet Turkish apricots (optional)
- handful chopped coriander
- Plain yoghurt and desiccated coconut for serving

Instructions:

1. First, heat oil in a pot and sauté onion for 5 to 8 minutes until soft.

2. Season chicken, add to pot and brown all over. Add ginger, garlic and turmeric and fry for a further 2 minutes.

3. Stir through spices and fry until sizzling and fragrant, stirring to coat meat with spices. Add curry leaves and stir in tomato paste, all the tomato, potatoes and stock. Season.

4. Cover and simmer for 25 to 30 minutes over a low medium heat.

5. Combine coconut milk and saffron (if using) and add to pot with apricots (if using).

6. Next, simmer uncovered for a further 10 to 15 minutes.

7. Stir in coriander and serve with a dollop of yoghurt and a sprinkling of desiccated coconut.

Chicken with Peas and Bacon

Serving Size: 4

Cooking Time: 1 Hour 35 Minutes

Ingredients:

- 2 Tbsp olive oil
- 1 onion, chopped
- 4 rashers bacon, cut into strips
- 1 ¾ Lb chicken pieces
- ½ Cup dry white wine
- ½ Cup chicken stock
- 1 Tbsp fresh sage, finely chopped
- ¾ Lb frozen green peas
- salt and freshly ground black pepper

Instructions:

1. Preheat the oil in a frying pan over high heat. Add the onion and bacon. Then, cook, stirring constantly for a few minutes approximately until the onion is soft, then remove onion and bacon and reserve.

2. Add the chicken in batches, turning often until the chicken is browned evenly.

3. Add the wine, stock, bacon and onion mixture and sage and bring to the boil.

4. Next, Reduce the heat and simmer for 20 minutes.

5. Then, add the peas and cook uncovered for a further 5 minutes, or until the peas are soft.

6. Lastly, season with black pepper and salt to taste and serve with mash or rice.

Chicken Korma

Serving Size: 4-6

Cooking Time: 1 Hour 45 Minutes

Ingredients:

- 4 chicken breasts
- 1 Cup yoghurt
- 2 tsp crushed garlic
- 2 tsp crushed ginger
- 2 medium onion, finely chopped
- 1 tsp paprika
- 2 tsp peanut or sunflower oil
- 1 tsp poppy seeds
- Seeds of 2 peeled cardamom pods
- 1 tsp turmeric
- 1 tsp cumin powder
- 1 tsp coriander powder
- 1 tsp chilli powder
- 2 bay leaves
- 1 Cup coconut milk
- 1 tsp salt or to taste
- 1 tsp lemon juice
- 4 Tbsp fresh coriander, chopped

Instructions:

1. Place chicken in bowl and marinate in the yoghurt, one teaspoon each of the garlic and ginger, half the onion and the paprika for a few hours or overnight.

2. Heat oil in a large heavy pan and sauté the dry spices until the seeds pop.

3. Add the remaining onion, garlic and ginger and sauté for 3 minutes.

4. Add chicken mixture with the marinade, the turmeric, cumin powder, coriander powder and chilli powder and bay leaves.

5. Add the coconut milk, then simmer until the chicken is cooked, about 45 minutes.

6. Season with salt, add the lemon juice and fresh coriander leaves, and simmer for another 10 minutes or until the coriander has blended into the korma.

7. Garnish with fresh coriander. Lastly, serve with basmati rice.

8. Tip: Be careful cautiously not to add too much salt. Sprinkle the korma with toasted slivered almonds for a special touch.

Beer and Chicken Pies

(The beer can be substituted with good quality chicken stock)

Serving Size: Makes 6 pies

Cooking Time: 1 Hour 15 Minutes

Ingredients:

- Oil, for frying
- 4 chicken breast fillets, diced
- salt and milled pepper
- 3 sticks celery, chopped
- 2 leeks, rinsed and sliced
- ½ packet mushrooms, sliced
- 1 Tbsp butter
- 2 Tbsp flour
- ½ Cup beer
- ½ Cup cream
- 1 roll shortcrust pastry, defrosted
- 1 roll puff pastry, defrosted
- 1 egg, lightly beaten

Instructions:

1. Heat oil in a large pot.

2. Add chicken, season and fry until golden.

3. Add celery, leeks and mushrooms and fry.

4. Add butter to pot to melt.

5. Sprinkle flour over and stir to coat meat and vegetable, then fry for 2 minutes.

6. Stir in beer and cream and simmer for 7 to 10 minutes, until slightly thickened.

7. Cool.

8. Line 6 x ⅔ Cups ovenproof ramekins with roll out shortcrust pastry.

9. Divide chicken mixture among dishes and cover with circles of puff pastry.

10. Crimp side using a for and refrigerate for 15 minutes.

11. Brush with egg and bake at 392°F for 20 to 25 minutes until pastry is golden.

Parsley and Parmesan Crumbed Chicken

Serving Size: 2

Cooking Time: 1 Hour 5 Minutes

Ingredients:

- 4 chicken breasts
- plain flour for coating
- ¾ Cup dry breadcrumbs
- ½ Cup freshly grated parmesan
- ½ Cup fresh parsley
- 1 egg, lightly beaten
- 2 Tbsp milk
- ¼ Cup oil

Instructions:

1. Flatten the chicken breast fillets between 2 sheets of plastic wrap with a meat mallet or rolling pin and coat in flour.

2. Combine the parmesan, breadcrumbs and parsley in a bowl.

3. Mix the egg and milk in a separate bowl.

4. Coat the fillets by dipping them first into the egg mixture and then into the crumb mixture. Press the crumb mixture firmly onto the chicken and leave in the refrigerator for 30 minutes.

5. Heat the oil in your frying pan over medium heat. Add two of the chicken breasts at a time and fry for 10 to 12 minutes, turning until the breasts are cooked through.

6. Serve with slices of lemon and starch of choice.

Sweat and Sour Chicken with Stick Rice

Serving Size: 4

Cooking Time: 1 Hour 30 Minutes

Ingredients:

- 4 chicken breasts
- salt and milled pepper
- Sauce:
- 1 onion
- 1 ½ inch ginger, strips
- 1 packet pineapple chunk
- 1 green pepper, cut into chunks
- 2 Tbsp tomato sauce
- ¼ Cup juice of lime
- ¼ Cup sugar
- ¾ Cup water
- 2 tsp cornflour in solution
- steamed rice

Instructions:

1. Cut chicken into pieces and season.

2. Fry chicken in a pan until brown. Set aside.

3. Cut the onion into chunks and lightly fry, ginger, pineapple and green pepper, vegetables.

4. Mix and simmer with remaining ingredients until sauce thickens.

5. Toss chicken in sauce to reheat.

6. Serve with steamed rice.

Bonus Recipes

Duck with Orange Marmalade Glaze

Serving Size: 6-8

Cooking Time: 2 Hour

Ingredients:

- 4 ½ Lb duck
- 1 onion, peeled and halves
- 2 sticks celery, cut in half
- 1 Tbsp soft butter
- salt and pepper to taste
- ½ tsp ground ginger
- 9 ½ oz orange marmalade
- ¼ Cup (or 3 tots) orange liqueur

Instructions:

1. First, clean the duck and pat dry with paper towels. Place the onion and celery inside the cavity of the duck. Spread butter over the skin of the duck and season with salt, pepper and ginger.

2. Place duck in a roast holder and position duck on the grid of the kettle braai, or place directly on the grid (fit a drip pan beneath the duck to catch all the juices and fat).

3. Cover and cook for about 1 ½ hours.

4. To make the glaze, heat the marmalade and liqueur in a saucepan and stir until well combined.

5. Next, during the last 30 minutes of cooking, baste the duck with the glaze about 3 times.

6. Remove duck from roast holder and allow to stand for 5 minutes before carving. Serve with baked potatoes and fresh vegetables.

Ostrich Pie

Serving Size: 4-6

Cooking Time: 1 Hour 20 Minutes

Ingredients:

- 4 tsp olive oil
- 1 onion, finely chopped
- 1 packet diced streaky bacon
- 1 packet seasoned ostrich goulash
- 4 tsp malt or cider vinegar
- 1 bay leaf, 4 whole cloves
- 1 Cup water
- 2 Tbsp cornflour
- 2 eggs
- 1 Cup milk
- 1 Cup sunflower oil
- 1 ½ Cups flour
- 4 tsp baking powder

Instructions:

1. Heat olive oil in a large pan, fry onion until brown and bacon until crispy.

2. Add seasoned ostrich goulash to pan and fry until brown.

3. Add malt or cider vinegar, bay leaf, cloves and water.

4. Next, season to taste, cover with a lid and lower heat so the meat gently simmers for about 30 minutes or until it falls apart. Add water to keep meat covered.

5. Remove meat and shred with a fork.

6. Then, mix cornflour with small amount of water to create a paste, then whisk into pan and boil for 2 minutes.

7. Spoon meat and mixture from pan into an oven-safe dish and mix.

8. Cool completely.

9. Whisk together eggs and 1 cup each milk and sunflower oil.

10. Combine flour, baking powder and a pinch of salt.

11. Add milk mixture to flour mixture, to create a thin and runny batter.

12. Spoon batter over filing and bake at 356°F for 30 minutes or until golden brown.

Cassoulet

Serving Size: 8

Cooking Time: 3 Hours 30 Minutes

Ingredients:

- 1 Lb haricot beans (small white beans), soaked
- overnight in cold water, then drained
- 1 Lb Toulouse sausages (or garlic sausages)
- 1 Lb boneless lamb, 1 Lb boneless pork, each cut into 5cm cubes
- 1 large onion finely chopped; 1 Tbsp crushed garlic
- 4 tomatoes, peeled, seeded and chopped
- 1 ¼ Cups chicken stock
- 1 bouquet garni
- 1 Cup fresh breadcrumbs
- 5 Tbsp oil, for frying, 1 litre water, salt and black pepper

Instructions:

1. Simmer the beans in a saucepan in ¼ gallon of water for 60 minutes, add 1 tsp salt and leave to soak in the water.

2. Prick each sausage and fry them over medium heat for 20 minutes or until they are browned.

3. Season the lamb and the pork with the salt and pepper and in the same pan, fry the lamb with the pork in batches until browned, adding a little extra oil as needed, and set aside.

4. Next, add the onion and garlic to the pan and cook until soft. Stir in the tomatoes and cook for 3 minutes more.

5. Drain the beans, reserving the liquid and place a quarter of the beans in a large casserole. Then, top with a third of the sausages, meat and the tomato and onion mixture.

6. Continue layering in this manner ending with a layer of beans. Add the bouquet garni and pour over the stock to just cover.

7. Cover the casserole and bake in the oven at 356°F for 2 hours.

8. Check and if a little dry, add a little of the reserved bean liquid as needed. Sprinkle over the breadcrumbs, pressing them down to moisten them.

9. Carry on cooking uncovered for 20 minutes until the breadcrumbs are nicely browned.

Conclusion

Hopefully, you have been able to advance somewhat into the art of preparing a meat dish, and you have left your guest with a good impression. The book wasn't necessarily directed at only beginners but was meant to provide a foundation to develop off. The book was designed and formatted so that you could continue to use it as a source of reference.

While you worked through the book, you were also encountering cultural diversity which helps provide a sense of adventure and of exploring something new. It was meant to be a fun journey and made the encounter insightful and informative.

Once you have worked through this cookbook, you would have realized that cooking meat dishes can be rather fun. So, if you would like to satisfy your appetite for further learning, then you might consider the other cookbooks from this publisher.

About the Author

Ivy's mission is to share her recipes with the world. Even though she is not a professional cook she has always had that flair toward cooking. Her hands create magic. She can make even the simplest recipe tastes superb. Everyone who has tried her food has astounding their compliments was what made her think about writing recipes.

She wanted everyone to have a taste of her creations aside from close family and friends. So, deciding to write recipes was her winning decision. She isn't interested in popularity, but how many people have her recipes reached and touched people. Each recipe in her cookbooks is special and has a special meaning in her life. This means that each recipe is created with attention and love. Every ingredient carefully picked, every combination tried and tested.

Her mission started on her birthday about 9 years ago, when her guests couldn't stop prizing the food on the table. The next thing she did was organizing an event where chefs from restaurants were tasting her recipes. This event gave her the courage to start spreading her recipes.

She has written many cookbooks and she is still working on more. There is no end in the art of cooking; all you need is inspiration, love, and dedication.

Author's Afterthoughts

I am thankful for downloading this book and taking the time to read it. I know that you have learned a lot and you had a great time reading it. Writing books is the best way to share the skills I have with your and the best tips too.

I know that there are many books and choosing my book is amazing. I am thankful that you stopped and took time to decide. You made a great decision and I am sure that you enjoyed it.

I will be even happier if you provide honest feedback about my book. Feedbacks helped by growing and they still do. They help me to choose better content and new ideas. So, maybe your feedback can trigger an idea for my next book.

Thank you again

Sincerely

Ivy Hope

Printed in Great Britain
by Amazon

33398218R00071